FAIRY TALES FOR HOPELESS GIRLS

RENA JOY

2026

Fairy Tales for Hopeless Girls copyright © 2025 by Rena Joy.
All rights reserved. No part of this book may be used or reproduced in any manner whatsoever without written permission except in the case of brief quotations embodied in critical articles and reviews.

For more poetry from Rena Joy:
TikTok @renajoypoetry
Instagram @renajoypoetry
www.renajoypoetry.com

Cover art and design: Jacinta Kay | @creativewannabe_.
Edited: Shelby Leigh.
Proofreader: Amanda Matwie.
Published by Amy Smith Publishing.

FAIRY TALES FOR HOPELESS GIRLS
Trade Paperback: 978-1-0690381-5-9.
EPUB: 978-1-0690381-6-6.
Published in Canada.
Printed in Canada / United States of America.

1. POETRY / Women Authors 2. POETRY/ General
10 9 8 7 6 5 4 3 2 1

ATTENTION: SCHOOLS AND BUSINESSES
Amy Smith books are available at quantity discounts with bulk purchase for educational, business, or sales promotional use. For information, please email amysmithbookpublishing@gmail.com.

Damaged, broken, unlovable—these are the lies the hopeless tell themselves because those who promised us a happy ending stole our choice, our voice and sometimes our will to live. But we are more than our trauma. We are truth seekers, cycle breakers, and warriors taking back what was stolen from us: a life worth living.

Fairy Tales for Hopeless Girls is a poetry collection about becoming yourself, loving yourself, and rewriting the false stories that have kept you small. Broken into five parts, this book is a path to where hope can thrive.

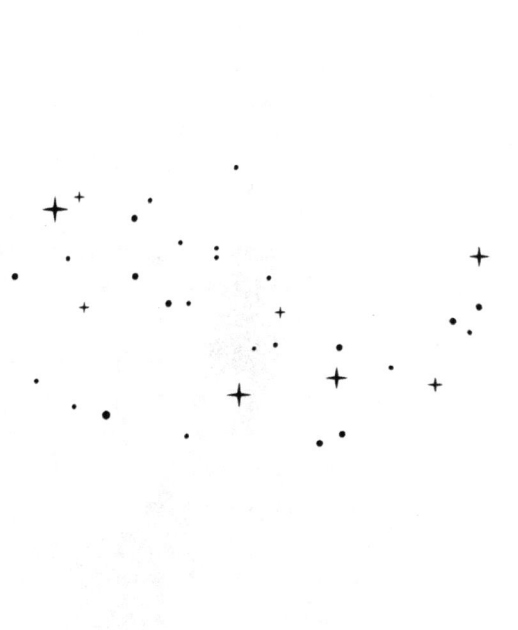

To my love: may you never be a hopeless girl.

Dear Reader,

If you're new to my work, welcome. If you're already a reader, thank you for the continued support. I'm an adoptee from foster care. While this collection isn't specifically about being an adoptee, my life experiences have shaped my point of view, just like your life experiences have shaped yours. Some of our experiences have created false stories that stop us from being the best version of ourselves. For me, some of those false stories include thinking I'm unlovable, unworthy of joy and success, and that I must act a certain way to be liked. This collection is about the false stories we are told and hold onto. My hope for you is that by the end of this book, you'll be able to start putting your harmful stories to rest.

XO
Rena

Content Warnings

Suicidal Ideation
Sexual Abuse
Attempted Sexual Assault
and Violence

These topics are touched upon in this book. In most cases, the poems are not graphic. Please take care, dear reader.

Contents

Hopeless	1
Godmother Promises	21
Crumbling Tower	41
Villain Era	81
Happily	119

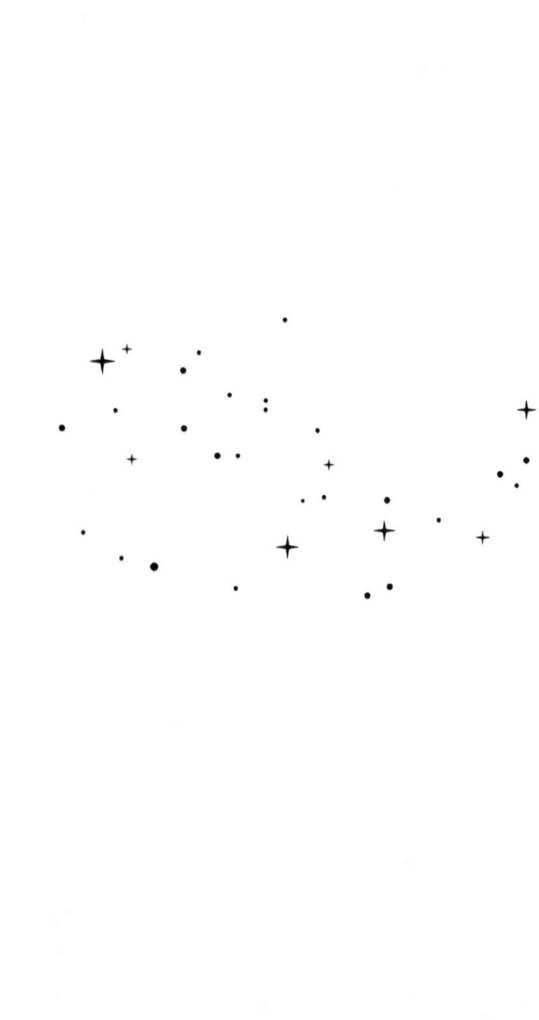

Hopeless

Hopeless Girl

I'm a hopeless girl
because hoping for change
and believing in fairy tales
didn't change my fate.

Doing the ugly thing,
the hateful thing,
the wicked thing,
finally set me free.

Defying Boys

My brother once locked me
in the back of an old school bus.
I didn't panic.
I didn't try the door I heard him lock.
Instead, I took in the dark space—
the mishmash of pillows and ropes
and garbage stuffed under seats.
I made myself small (I was used to that part)
and pushed through a slit in the floor like a mouse.
It didn't take long
to secure my freedom,
at least for the day.

Queen

My name used to mean beloved—
then it changed to queen.
It's suiting because royal women
are required to act a certain way.
Even in a place of privilege,
they still have their choices stripped.

What woman hasn't felt this way at least once?

The Day I Almost Died

It was the day I almost died and
I'm trying to understand through her eyes.
I'm not sure what prompted her actions that night,
although I know why she felt hopeless.

I'm not sure there was a concrete plan
beyond snatching the pills from her dad's dresser
(they had been calling to her for weeks).

I'm not sure she really wanted to die
but it felt like the only way to get a witness to her pain.
Still, she ended up alone in her friend's basement,
swallowing pills with a vodka chaser,
begging the reaper to do his job.

When You Feel Like an Impostor

In my dreams,
I can fly
but when I'm ready to launch,
I stumble—
get caught up in telephone wires.
In a space where anything is possible,
I still can't seem to soar.

Purple Couch

When we explore the abandoned gravel pit,
Queenie looks back to make sure
I haven't wandered off,
lost in a brain that doesn't always
want to be here,
but the empty woods aren't alarming.

Then she's gone, nose deep in crunchy leaves,
tracking a deer or last night's howling foxes.
I trip over fallen trees
and wade through thigh-high thistles,
replacing my skin with nettles and burrs.
An owl hoots at the approaching darkness.
I holler back—there are no limits in the forest—
only beauty and endless air
that never seem to catch in my rib cage.

Queenie bounds back,
hearing an approaching truck
and the clang of a gate opening.
I reassure her that momma doesn't need protecting
but she stands at attention just in case.

RENA JOY

At home, she climbs into my lap,
letting the day sigh out of her.
I pick at the slivers lodged in my palm—
tomorrow's proof I'm still breathing.

In bed, Queenie's body is pressed to mine.
I'm her home—a place to be loved and nurtured.
The kind of safety I search for
on my therapist's hardback purple couch.

Rapunzel's Closed Adoption

Do you remember how hard you cried
the first time you were separated from your mom?
She probably hugged you.
Reassured you you would be okay.

Rapunzel lost her parents.
She wasn't allowed to feel scared
because a witch stole her in the night
and whisked her off to an ivory tower.
For that, she should be grateful.

Send Me a Sign

I spot a pair of eagles
nesting together on my drive home.

It feels like a sign
to trust my partner.
To recall why
we said I do forever.

I'm flooded with memories—the yellow
and orange roses that delighted me.
The letter that confessed your love.
The support that helped me chase my dream.

I want us to be enough,
to carry me through the splitting rage,
the moments I'm convinced I wasn't made for love.

But I'm not sure
happily ever after is for me
when I keep dreaming of escape.

Solitude

I enjoy solitude
because it's easier to disconnect
than to face feeling loved.

Lost Girl

A backtrack of frogs
sing a lullaby.
I'm at peace,
lying out on the balcony
with a perfect cup of comfort.

I sip and savour
in tune with nature.

A memory flash,
a buzzing
drowns out the trees, the birds, and lover frogs.
I'm a prisoner to a clown melody,
consumed by the chaos of distant memories.

A cold breeze
prickles and pokes.
My vison blurs with tears
and I can taste their saltiness.
I keep turning the knob in my head,
reaching for familiar smells, sights, and sounds.
But not even a warm cuppa and
the safety of nature's whisper
can ground me now.

Grey

My father thinks
I never have anything positive to say
but he's the one who taught me
the world is grey.

Dead Grass is My Haven

Trauma carved ruts in my brain.
I'm trying hard to backfill worn paths,
so that maybe the grass will grow,
the flowers will bloom and the bees will return.

But I'm unsure,
and tired,
and the long way around
is through an unlit path.
Treading on dead grass feels safer.

Heirloom Tomatoes

I don't like gardening—prepping beds
and toiling over the soil, as thought worms
and other pests creep under the surface.
I never seem to remember to nurture my tender seedlings.
I'm either too much water, or not enough.

I dread the daily weeding carried out in silence.
Doubts begin to sprout as
my self-worth competes
for space and sunlight.

Then there is the harvest,
twisting life from vines.
Tomatoes are destined for the cutting board,
or a pot of boiling water,
it feels cruel to be sustained by such violence.

I wonder if my first mother likes gardening.
Or if she, too, grieves for the lost family
she'll never pass plants on to.

Allure

Fairy tales are swirling
in your head again.
Pulling you from
building a life full of meaning.
It's easier to believe in stories
than to re-envision the life you're living.

The World Is My Oyster

I wonder who I would've become
if I had been loved from the start.
Would I feel safe asking for help?
Would I sink into hugs, unafraid they would end?
Would I know your love is real
and not my delusional longing to belong?

Would I be okay believing in fairy tales?

The Goldfish Bowl Is Out of Oxygen

You ask me if I'm good and
I have no answer for you.
I'm waiting for the cover of night
to fill my head with all the reasons I'm wrong.
To show my body to never leave
fight or flight.
Forever stuck in a loop,
like goldfish swimming circles for owners
who no longer notice them.

The tank is cloudy and dirty.
I'm not always okay
but I want to be happy.
Let me be free from this glass house,
to scrub the dirt from my tongue and throat;
to taste the freedom of a fresh start.

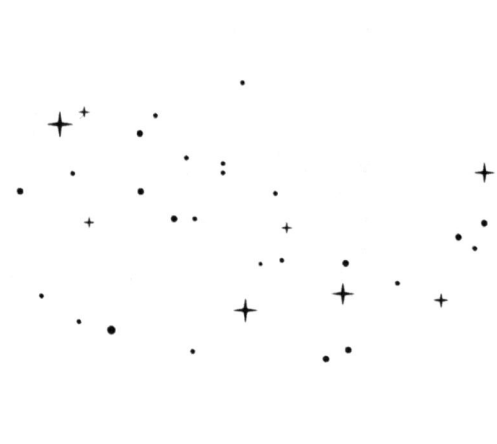

Godmother Promises

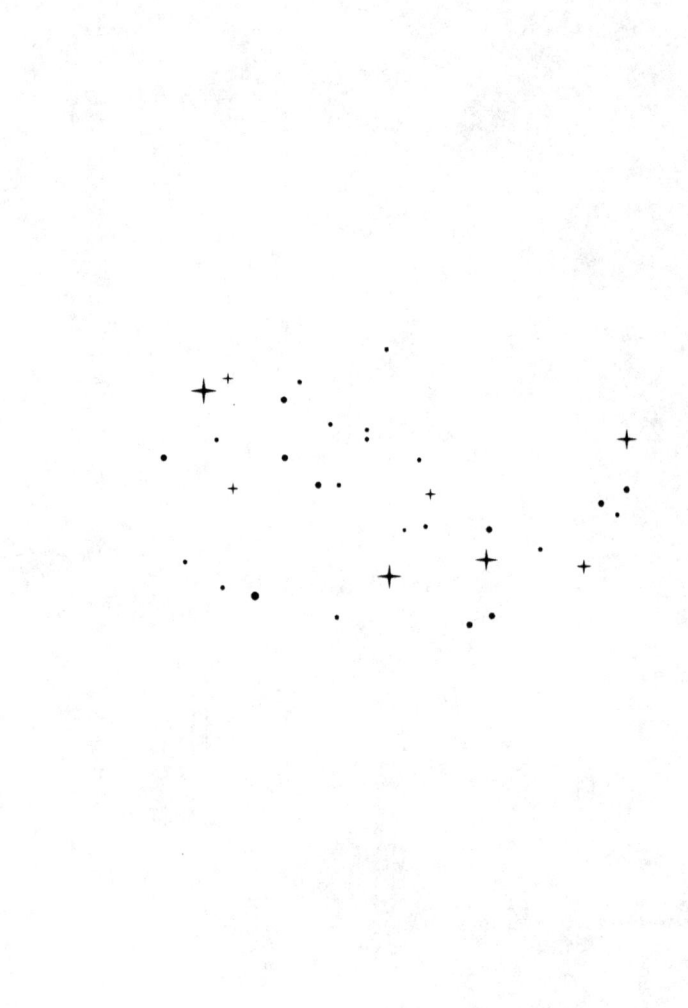

Love You to Neptune and Beyond

My love is here on my chest,
brewing a storm with her tiny fists.
Stirring inside me an ancestral grief
for all the daughters never truly loved.
For all the daughters showered in cursed glass.
Doubting their needs and desires.

My love deserves the moon and the stars
and the planets yet discovered.
So did you.

Goldilocks' Future

Another day.
Another story of a goldilocks
who would've been safer
eating porridge with a family of bears
vs. drinking coffee with the neighbourhood nice guy.

I'm one of the good ones, he says.
But does he even know the colour of her eyes?
I'm one of the kind ones, he says.
As long as the conversation goes his way.
Not all men, he says.
Remaining silent when his bro crosses the line.

Goldilocks knew the animals who harmed her,
while the world stood by demanding answers: Are you sure?
What were you wearing? Did you report them?

Goldilocks' only mistake was believing
she had found a safe place to exist—to nourish,
to relax, to restore.
But selfish claws ripped her from hopeful dreams,
forever shifting her reality.

Goldilocks would've been safer with the bear.
She doesn't want her daughter to be safer with a bear.

Why Therapy?

I can escape without ever leaving the room—a skill
I hope my daughter never needs to survive.

Would You Rescue Me?

My mother said
to the man I married,
I was mostly a good girl.
Like I had been keeping secrets.
Like my love didn't know me.

But what the hell did she know
about the daughter she once called a whore—
a sinner girl, but it wasn't me doing the sinning
the night she caught me on the downstairs couch.
Intoxicated and naïve, I was the perfect peach
for a prince trying to take things too far.

-my mother, unintended rescuer

Unworthy

The pressure is building inside my head.
Maybe I should quit.
Embrace the loser
I'm destined to be.

But father, I can't let you win,
so I'll keeping working
on this self hate you gave me.

Pickle

She is rummaging through the fridge again
like the contents can cure
the emptiness taking root in her gut.

She reaches for the pickle jar
and a memory appears
of grandma's house,
eating dills together
as an afternoon snack.

They laugh over the ridiculousness
of a deep-fried pickle,
but they would both try it if they had a chance.

Now it's too late
because Grandma is gone
and the pickle jar won't open.

Why the hell does life have to be like this?

She shoves the pickle jar back in the fridge
and slams the door closed.

Sorry, Grandma, sorry.

Keep the Faith

Some of you believe in God—you're only given
as much as you can handle.
Some of you trust in the universe—life will be
as it should.

But I'm not about to drop to my knees
and take another mouthful of dirt
from the grave life keeps digging,
when I can't even believe in myself.

Slow Season

I don't want winter to come
but she always does.
I'm forced to slow down
and reflect on how life has been.

In those reflections, there are shadows.
I'm not sure if I'm stable enough
to invite them in,
take off their coat
and get cozy with them by the pellet stove.

There is a 50/50 chance the shadow will either
hold my hand, or coax me outside
to walk across a melting pond.

Brothers Grimm

Tonight, I curl up with the Brothers Grimm Fairy Tales.
I read about all the girls
who were saved by the prince, the woodsman,
the godmother.
Tale after tale filled with misled girls
who accepted their fate.

I can't blame them.

I once dreamt of being Belle from Beauty and the Beast.
I wanted to be whisked away from my father
and lost in magic and books.
A place where real monsters
couldn't reach me.

I. Inner Child

Maybe you feel abandoned
but your inner child
never stopped loving you.
She was stuck
in the ick the world
couldn't stop spewing.
A tale of never enough.

II. Inner Child

She's enough.
You're enough.
As a pair, you're ready
to ascend to the height of everything
you're meant to be.

God, Are You Listening?

I'm writing a letter to God
because praying doesn't seem to work.
How great would it be to get a handwritten letter?
I doubt he gets anything fun.
Maybe an inbox of complaints and pleas and ramblings
from questioning girls.
Maybe this will grab his attention.
Maybe I'm being selfish for wanting a relationship with
god not born out of fear.
Okay, here I go.

To God.
Dear God.
Hi God, it's me.
I have so much to say.
My hand is already aching with the weight of it all.
I'm afraid you are going to tell me
I've only been given as much as I can handle,
even though young me holding a bottle of pills,
would disagree.
But that isn't why I'm writing.

As you know, Grandma died today.

The last time I saw her, we held hands,
we locked eyes, and she smiled.
I said, I love you.
She said, I love you.
I knew that would be the last time we saw each other.
Still, I was hoping for a miracle.
That somehow, she would beat age.
Be the exception to your rule.
Now I have to keep on existing
with no adoptive family left to love me.

Maybe you love me, but I wouldn't know
because you never answer back.

Bye!
Love?
Sincerely,

Me

P.S. Do you love me? Send me a sign.

*Inspired by Judy Blume's novel, *Are You There God? It's Me, Margaret*.

Daddy's Little Girl

Husband,

Please don't make me believe you will
always love our daughter,
only to tear her heart out.
Please don't tell her she can do anything
while stealing her will to live.
Please don't check for monsters under her bed
only to become one.
Please don't ever be a reason
she doesn't feel safe.
Please don't ever make me choose
between my love for her, and my love for you
(you won't win).

Please.
Never.
Stop.
Loving.
Her.

Sending Love

When I see a shooting star,
or maybe it's a satellite,
my kid heart leaps.
Make a wish.
It doesn't seem to matter how much healing I've done.
Little me sends love into the universe
with the hope it will return.
But lately, I've been hoping
my wish will find some other little girl
in desperate need of love.

I. Old Enough

I'm old enough to know:
you will not be believed.
You will be picked apart.
You will be blamed.
But I hope you know in those moments:
you are not the broken one.

II. Old Enough

I'm also old enough to know:
You will be believed.
You will be held.
You will be supported.
I hope sooner rather than later.
Please don't stop speaking.
We need your voice.

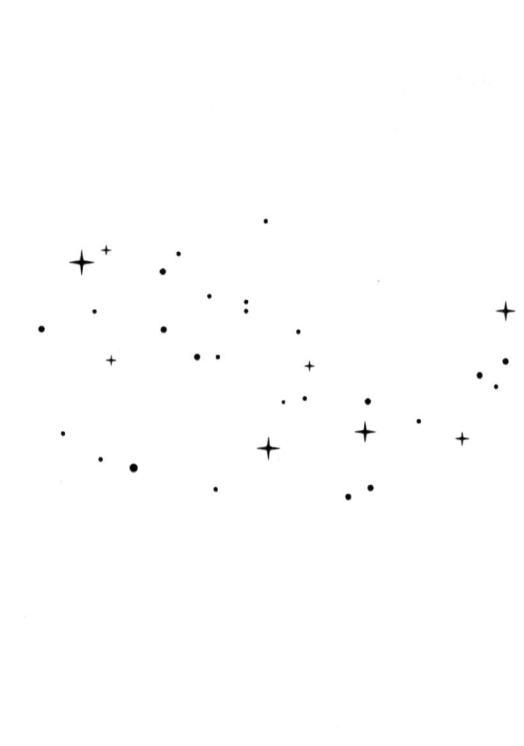

Crumbling Towers

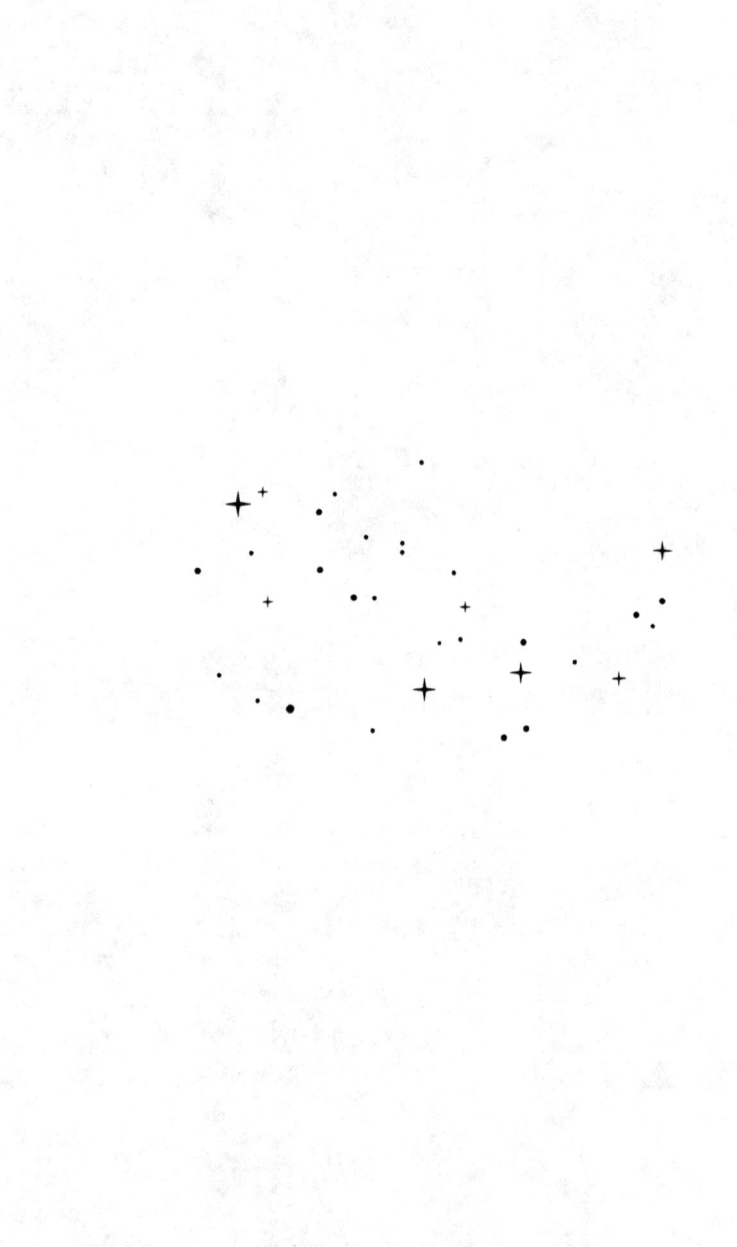

RENA JOY

Rapunzel's Awakening

Knowing yourself is a birthright
Rapunzel was never granted
because a witch stole her in the night
and locked her history behind what's best.

Best not to bring up the past.
Best not to ask questions.
Best to be grateful for the life she has.
Best to feel nothing at all.

Best.
Best.
Best.

Best doesn't stop the tears
after mother has gone to bed.
Best doesn't soothe thoughts of leaving life behind
long before she's done living.
Best hasn't mended her fragmented heart,
or provided answers to stop its ache.
Rapunzel is not her best.
She doesn't know who best is.

Every Girl, Every Woman, Has a Story

I remember the time the neighbourhood pervert was
soliciting teen girls through his mail boy. (age 13)
I remember the time at the mall approached by a man,
old enough to be my grandfather.
He offered me his apartment. (age 15)
I remember the time the neighbourhood boys joked
about raping me. (age 16)
I remember the time at the bus stop getting hit on.
He could've been my grandfather too. (age 17)
I remember the time my cousin left me with her friend
and locked herself in her room
with her children. (age 18)
I remember the taxi driver waggling his brows.
Being with a group of women didn't make me
feel safer. (age 19)
I remember the time I was stalked
in the mall parking lot. (age 19)
I remember the time I was stopped on the sidewalk in the
middle of the day and solicited for sex work. (age 20)
I remember the time my supervisor
put his hands on me. (age 22)
I remember the time walking home from work
and being chased around a man's car
until he gave up and drove off. (age 22)

By the time I hit puberty, I already knew what predators were like because
I remember the time after baptising the dead. (age 12)
I remember the time I was left with a cousin. (age 12)
I remember the time I trusted my handsy father. (age 13)

I remember the time before I knew what sexual abuse was and the time after knowing what they did was wrong with no recourse.

Too many times.

13 times between the ages of 12-22 before I lost count.
12/13 were adult men.
1/13 was a teen girl.

I didn't deserve this. We don't deserve this.

Mirror Mirror On the Stained Wall

Mirror mirror
in front of me.
Mirror my words,
back to me.
Shake me awake;
make me see
Prince Charming is nothing
but a dick
with a massive ego.

RENA JOY

She Never Cries Wolf

I want to cry out loud,
not while I wash the day's gunk
from my overworked body.
Not while I lie in bed,
waterboarding my pillow.
Not while I rock my silent screams
to the rhythm of my husband's snores.
I don't want to be alone in my pain.
But what if I let my grief be known
and you still don't hear me?

Hi, God.

It's just me, again.
I'm sitting on the couch
writing sad girl poetry.
I'm wondering if you exist.
If you're real,
can you tell me
how my grandma is doing?

Star Sign

I should've been a Gemini.
Two worlds. Two different girls.
Instead, I'm a woman on fire
with her bow at the ready.

I'm always at the ready,
to strike down any perceived threat.

Lately, my arms have started to ache.
Maybe it's time to put down my bow.

Even a girl on fire
needs space to breathe.

Let the Odds Be In Your Favour

You're breathing,
deep and steady now.
Scaling beanstalks.
Reconciling with your past selves.

No longer living a split life
on magical blood,
or spinning tales
to make it to another day.
You're stepping out to heal.
Please step back in.
Sing your mockingjay tune.

RENA JOY

When They Ask for Receipts

What happened to you
was real, even if you kept it all inside.
What happened to you
wasn't okay, even if others couldn't see it.
You have to be your own source of truth.
You can show up with evidence,
but denial is a tricky thing.
Do you really need to prove your pain
when those already in your corner didn't ask for receipts?

It's a Girl!

I wasn't always at war with my father.
Somewhere along the way,
he changed the rules.
I became unlovable.
Maybe it was the day I beat him at a game of 21.
Or maybe it was my inability to keep my mask on
and my rambling mouth shut.
Or maybe when he came home from a year long
absence to discover I had developed breasts.
I don't know what I did wrong,
beyond being born a girl.

Gretel Stopped Searching for Breadcrumbs

I no longer hate my father.
I'm indifferent, and
in some ways, that's worse
than feeling anger.

Before, there was grief
and rage and hope to repair.
A dream where I could regain
the love I thought I once had,
back before I became
a troublesome girl.

But there was nothing
left worth fighting for
when the cost was my one life.

In Another Life My Mother and I Understand Each Other

My mother left for another life
a province over.
She said she didn't know if I wanted her around,
but she's asking the wrong question.

She can't see the bridge between us
needs reinforcement,
not a complete teardown.

If we could get to a place
where we told the truth,
maybe visiting wouldn't
be a bumpy ride,
but a direct link
to two hearts capable of repair.

A mother and daughter
wanting to know each other.

Glass Eye; Hard Heart

Do you know the tale of the boy
who got a glass splinter in his eye and heart?
He no longer viewed the world
as safe and beautiful
until the tears from his lover
made him whole again.

While love can do wonders,
it is not enough to close wounds
a lover isn't willing to work on themselves.
Their grief is not your glue
but a sign to do the work,
while they're still willing to hold your hand.

The Little Mermaid

When the world is too quiet,
the thoughts pour in.
I fill the noise with junk and thingamabobs
and if I'm lucky, laughter.

When the world is too loud,
my body aches for nothingness.
I slip away underwater
missing sunken treasures
to deal with tidal waves.

When the world is just right,
I take it by storm,
riding this high,
forgetting all that is wrong with me.
I want to stay up,
but the high of a prince's almost kiss
only lasts so long.
I come crashing down to yesterday.
No amount of fairytale bliss
or sea witch wishes
will fix my past.
Healing is up to me.

RENA JOY

If only I could find a way to feel
that doesn't leave me voiceless and alone.
If only castles in the sky weren't so attractive.
If only… shut up world!
Life is here in the now.

Not the Silence You Were Looking For

In my home, the TV was always on.
The volume turned up
when I tried to speak.

You wanted my silence,
so I granted your wish when I walked away.
But it wasn't just my silence you craved—
it was the pain etched across my face.

RENA JOY

Fortune Cookie

I cracked open my future
to see what it may say:
a warning, a truth, a heartbreak?

I plucked the insides out,
while crunching on its shell.

"You are loved."
I am loved?

I toss my fortune
to my lover.

He cups the paper in his hands
as his eyes search my face.

"I love you."
I don't believe you.

He presses his hand into mine
and shows me his fortune: third time's the charm.

"I love you. I love you. I love you."

My heart flutters.
Maybe I should give love a chance.

Do Unto Others

You spend hours
picking worms from the sidewalk,
saving them from the last night's storm.
You're a lead foot
stopping to avoid the
frog in the road.

You're an endless bundle of support and breaks—
bringing home a fluffball, abandoned and scared,
or picking up the crooked tree for Christmas.

You spend hours being kind
to everyone and everything
but yourself.

-maybe it's time to show yourself some love

Why I Went No Contact

I was never going to thrive
in a place I had to earn my existence.

In Case She Didn't Know

It's Christmas.
I'm at my in-laws,
post sandwiches and cheesecake.
My little is playing on the floor.

I'm thinking about my grandparents, and
how visiting them felt like waking up
from a restful night, to be greeted with
sun on my face and the smell of a good day unfolding.

I tell my mother-in-law she's a good grandma,
as we make ourselves a cup of tea.
She flees from the kitchen
back to the rest of the family.
Perhaps she believes their company will stop my confession,
but I'm not uncomfortable with my feelings.

Her father never gives her compliments.
He isn't a cruel person.
His kids are supposed to just know
the good they are doing.

I wonder if she knows
that her home feels like being wrapped in a toddler hug
where their entire being sinks into you.

RENA JOY

I don't want her to wonder,
so I follow her to the living room
and repeat myself, "You're a good grandmother."
She throws herself in her chair.
"I like children," she says.

I think to myself,
my father liked children too—at least some.
I wasn't one of them, nor was my daughter.

Mother/Daughter

My mother and I have a habit
of not telling each other the whole truth.
Our feelings are hidden behind misty eyes.

I'm not sure how to fix this connection
when one of us believes in fairy tales,
and the other runs screaming from the wolf in the bed.

Ashes to Ashes

You've been reduced to ash
more times than you can count.
Maybe you've been waiting to fly,   to soar,   to climb
to the height of everything
you've yet been brave enough
to r e l e a s e.

Maybe you weren't
in need of a burning
but a hand
               to rise again.

I. Not Quite a Love Poem for Father's Day

I wish I could write
a happy poem for Father's Day
but I'm not like the other kids—
with a father who adored them,
with a father who cared enough
to hear about their day without
turning up the volume on the TV,
with a father who believed
women and girls had value.
I'm so damn jealous
I'll never be like the other kids,
loved by their father.

II. Not Quite a Love Poem for Father's Day

I'll never be like the other kids
but my daughter is growing up
the way I wished I did.
It's so damn healing
to see I picked better.
We're both loved by her father.

Eve and the Snake

In family therapy
I drew myself as a snake,
my father a gorilla,
my brother a bird because
it was the closest animal to heaven.

The therapist was pleased
I showed them what they wanted.
Me a villain, my father a protector,
but my bird brother
was the only one who ever looked out for me.

If I had been safe in that room,
I would've been a manatee.
But I wasn't an endangered species—
just a girl in danger—
a sea cow in desperate need of protection
from the predator home I was placed in,
not to be blamed for mankind's downfall.
I was a child.

I'm grown now.
In my new therapist's office
I think about the snake.

Perhaps it was telling me that one day
I would transform and shed the shame
I was never meant to wear.

Two Steps Forward, One Step Back

I'm healing

　

　　　　　　　while treading

　

in a tar pit of memories.

Liar, Liar on the Wall …

I looked into a magic mirror and it said,
"You are loved."
I searched her reflection
to see if the mirror was lying.
I can't tell anymore.
That's the best I can do today.

Taking a Chance on Love

You're like that all-night read
I didn't want to put down.
I secretly promised
my cursed heart
one more chapter,
then I'll rest, satisfied.

The sun arrived too quickly.
I needed to see the last page.
To know our happy ending.
Blurry eyed, I made it to the end
only to discover
part two hadn't been written.

A Pebble in His Shoe

I was bitten once by a wasp
after I hit its nest while cleaning up a rose bush.
They were protecting their home, and
when the pain subsided, I understood their rage.
Maybe that's why my father hated me.
He was protecting his family
from the riffraff, second-hand garbage, the orphan girl
his wife brought home. But my father wasn't a wasp;
I wasn't garbage.

Open the Box

I'm afraid of what I could become.
A voice wrapped around me in the middle of the night
when the shoulds go haywire.

I'm afraid my story is Pandora's box.
Life really was greener before I opened my
stupid mouth.

I'm afraid I'm rewiring my brain.
Becoming the woman
I could've been if I had love all along.

Mostly, I'm afraid all this healing won't be enough
to save my life.

Mother, You Had It All

Mother,
I know loss changed you.
It changed me too.
But I was a child left to grieve on my own, twice over.
You had a spouse, and a church,
and the resources to get help.
I had a teddy bear to collect my tears
and a book that asked if I was still a sister.

Did you ever think for a second
of the brother and sister I lost before I came to you?
Did they not count because they weren't your blood?
Didn't carry your last name?
Where was my comfort then?

I was their sister; I still am.
A closed adoption doesn't change that.
Maybe one day I'll find my lost siblings.
Hopefully, not at their graves.

Hi, God.

It's me, sad girl.
I'm wondering
if there is meaning
to all this healing.
If there is,
can you get to the point already?

He Took His Apology to the Grave

All I wanted from my father was—I'm sorry.
Sorry for being selfish.
Sorry for breaking your trust.
Sorry for not seeing you for you.

But in his eyes he was perfect.
In his eyes I was a mistake, a temptress.
For that reason, my forgiveness died with him.

Alice's Therapist is in Her Head Again

Alice is climbing down a rabbit hole.
Rung by rung, she spirals:

My friend won't hear me.
My mother won't show up.
My lover won't ever understand.

But what if, instead of disbelieving,
Alice gave them a chance
to be here for her?

Rapunzel Let Down Your Hair

Rapunzel became what her family needed—
a crumbling tower.
She tossed her long hair
for them to climb.

Strand by strand,
she fell apart
until she was brave enough
to exit through the trapdoor.

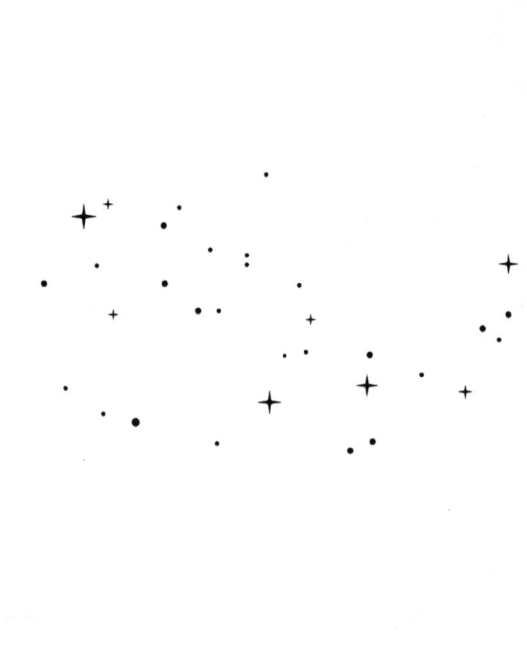

Villain Era

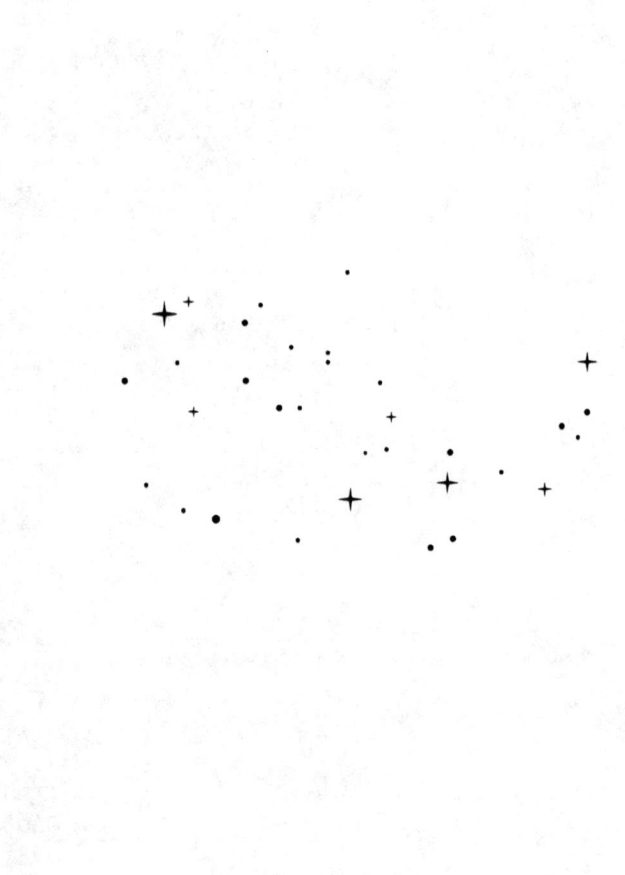

Jack & Jill

Grief and rage
went up the hill
to collect a pail of tears.
Grief fell down and stole his own life
and rage came tumbling after.

Briar Rose

I didn't visit you
on your deathbed,
and maybe that makes me
the hateful daughter.

I tried to rewrite our story
so many times.
I made believe that
you didn't harm me.

I tried to be someone else.
Loving you for mother's sake,
but my love for her
couldn't erase the chill from my bones.

I tried so damn hard
to remain asleep,
to never escape the briar patch.
I made believe that
struggling would only make my life worse.

Your cage of thorns—meant to protect you—
ripped me open,
stole my breath.
Your barbs broke your hold.

RENA JOY

In the end,
I couldn't forget
what you turned me into—
the wicked daughter
my mother may never forgive.

On This Day I Give Thanks

I'm not from the same family tree
as the man who raised me.
For that, I'm grateful.

Post-Apocalyptic

If tomorrow was the last day,
would life be any different?
Would I be less busy,
less lonely,
less hopeful?
Would I suddenly be present?
Would you?
Or would another me emerge,
whispering among the dead,
wearing a mask sewn
from the scars you left behind?
Would I change as I
embrace a new world order
where the likes of you
would be a happy meal
by the day's end?
Or is a barbed bat more my style?
Between fake smiles and red-hot
irons to faces,
you wouldn't dare
defy me (ovary status and all),
begging for a chance you never gave me.

This is the end;
kindness is dead.
Sweet release from expectation.

All I Got Was This Crappy Poem

I was made the family villain
yet still survived.

Turn the Cheek

I'm trying to be kind
to myself,
to everyone I meet.

Some of you
turn my kindness to rage.
I can feel a tingle in my chest.
Let them have it. They deserve it.
I rub my finger where my
what would Jesus do ring used to sit.

He took the abuse,
so I don't have to be a sacrificial lamb
for someone's hate.

Rumpelstiltskin

I find joy
in cracking a new journal
and picturing your head
doing the same,
as I unpack stories
you got to take to the grave,
leaving me holding
all the lies you spun.

A Worthy Villain

Maybe Rapunzel is a villain
for rejecting the only mother she could remember.
But she did the unthinkable anyway, escaped.
She became a master of her own life.

A Good Friday with a Dysfunctional Family

Your impending death
sat heavy on my chest—a stomping ground
of what ifs.
My stomach became a breeding ground
of knots—should I forgive?

I saw my mother's rage for the first time
as I let go of a fairytale dad.
A balancing act, me or them?
A decision I shouldn't have had to make.

In the end, I chose me
because no one else would.

No Forgives Left to Give

I forgave you when you hurt me.
I forgave you when you hurt me again.
I forgave you for your table-scrap love.

I forgave you.
I forgave you.
I forgave you.

I forgave you until
the words blurred
and forgiveness
lost all meaning.

As a mother now,
I can't forgive you anymore
because I finally understand
how easy it is to love your child.

Gap

I'm no longer silent
about things people
don't want to sit with.
They're too quick to the keyboard—
to blame, to shame, to silence.
Between their lines,
I've created space
to talk about the hard things.
Things people don't
want to understand—
too busy spewing their *not all*.
I'll keep reaching for your hand,
blasting open a gap for you
to talk about the things that hurt you.
They can't silence us all.

A Thought That Keeps Me Up at Night

If I don't tell,
will there be others?
Were there others?

When the Tomato Doesn't Fall Far from the Vine

My brother covered my bed in ashes
by flicking cigarettes butts from his window to mine.
I no longer slept with mine open despite the stifling heat.
I no longer left my room unlocked.
I was no longer permitted to just be.

All that time, I thought brothers were supposed to
protect their little sisters.
I was wrong.
Boys like to mimic their fathers.

RENA JOY

I Don't Know How Others Find Empathy for Abusers

Maybe because I wasted so many nights
trying to understand what I did wrong,
praying I could just be the daughter
my father could love.

Maybe because his hatred
almost ended my life.
It's not normal for a thirteen-year-old
to want to die.

Maybe the rage that has finally surfaced
like a dormant volcano
is tired of his side of the story.
I'm finally in a place I can call out the bullshit!
(He didn't love me; he didn't love himself.)

In this space, I don't judge me.
I hold my hand,
speak softly,
become the understanding I need.

The Snow Queen

Maybe she was the scapegoat for
a world turned cold,
shunning her as she aged.
No longer a trophy
to decorate their palace.

Reverse Cinderella

Two years after my brother's death,
my father left us to teach in another country.
Eventually, he returned in the middle of the night
to grace us with his presence before escaping
somewhere new.

He convinced my mother
to sell everything and chase him across the world,
only for him to abandon us again and return home.

Every day he was gone, I filled with rage.
How selfish can one person be?
It didn't matter his wife's and daughter's lives
were shattering. He kept on leaving.

On a day I was being a bit too difficult,
my mother screamed,
"What do you want me to do? Leave him?"
Yes.
But it wasn't my place to tell her to stop chasing love.

Crown

Everyone points fingers.
It's not she said/they said.
It's see/ignore/vilify.
It's easier to cast blame
than to face their own truth.
So give me a crown
and Ice Queen status.
I'd rather be a villain
in this story
than remain a damsel in distress.

Unlimited

When others want to limit you,
take up space.

                Take up the whole damn room;

                              squeeze them out the door.

E   x   p   a   n   d

like the universe you're meant to be.

The Labels We Carry

I don't belong here,
sorted by rags or riches
and inner complexes.

I don't belong here,
divided by feather boas
and souls untethered.

I don't belong here,
in depths or shallows
with no way to swim.

I don't belong here,
in pews or brothels
and hidden agendas.

I don't belong here;
neither do you.

The Selfless Girl

My family was hurting, and I shut them out.
I couldn't be there in the way they needed
without destroying myself.

They may never understand why I disappeared,
but I'll never understand where they went
when I stuffed my face with pills
and rocked my scared self to sleep
and soaked my pillow through.

I was alone when they had the world around them.
Now I can't be who they want—the selfless girl.
There is nothing left in me to give.

Wicked Witch of the West

Dorothy pulled a book from the shelf.
She sniffed the pages and flipped through
stories from far-off lands.
She was searching for her grandma's voice.
She lay back in bed.
Once upon a time, off to a good start.
The witch, her father's voice, invaded the story.
Stealing the spotlight like he tended to do.

Dorothy doesn't want his version of events
where women are either wicked or hopeless.
With grandma, there is an in-between place
where girls exist as whole beings capable of
being more than a prize.
She sits up in bed.
Go away.
But his version of the witch doesn't melt,
despite the tears streaming down Dorothy's face.

RENA JOY

Reconciling With My Past Self

Healing is knowing
I haven't always
been the best version of myself.

I have intentionally hurt others.
I have justified being petty
and thrown barbs disguised as jokes.

I have been a villain
in someone's story.

There is nothing left to say
except I'm sorry.
There is nothing left to show
except my changed ways.

Anger is a Normal Response to Being Harmed

If there is an after,
I hope
you're
a
burning   man.

Part Time Monster

My abuser was loved,
while he denied me
the safe affection I craved.
I was an outlet
for his lack of self-love.
To my brothers,
he was a hero.
I've accepted
he was different with them.
But to me, he will always be
the monster under my bed,
giving out just enough treats
to keep us all fooled.

Don't Be the Wolf Waiting in Grandma's Clothes

No is not an invite.
Compliance is not an invite.
Clothes are not an invite.
Reputation is not an invite.
Boyfriend status is not an invite.
Intoxication is not an invite.
Opportunity is not an invite
but a chance to act right.
The friend zone is not an invite;
change your mindset.
Vulnerability is not an invite.
Doing a favour is not an invite.
A date is not an invite
even if you pay.
Worth is not an invite;
that will never change.

The rules are simple:
My body. My choice.

My no is not a yes in disguise.
A yes is allowed to change.

RENA JOY

I'm not a princess waiting to be kissed awake,
or your reward for the taking.
Consent is king.
You know and I know what no means—hands off.
Guilt trip not needed.

Why Won't the World Just Stop?

The world keeps turning
because trauma causes wormholes.
Swallowing up memories,
delivering you to a time when
people expect more
than you can give.

We Are All Villains

We are all villains
in someone's story.
But are we brave enough to
repair what's worth saving?
Are we wise enough to
shed our past?
Are we willing to do the work
even when it hurts?

Bada Bing

You didn't know what was raging inside me,
only that I was hurting.
You didn't know this pain
almost consumed me, back before I had you.
I was stuck in time when no wasn't enough
and relations meant nothing.
Trust and hearts were broken in the worst way.

You greeted me with gifts — a bat,
and a car destined for crush.
You showed me the best spots
to let my rage flow through me
until I was out of breath and buzzing,
as though I had drunk an urn of espresso.

My grief took a knee
as fire cracked my ribs.
I let go — the shame, the doubt, my secrets —
like Elsa, the snow queen,
was motherfucking Negan,
a post-apocalyptic saviour.

The wounded me and the warrior me
rejoined,
reclaimed my body,
my choice.

RENA JOY

For a moment,
I pictured them splattered on the ground.
Justice for a jail cell,
they'll never know.

Like a Sister No More

I defended you
because I knew the broken
you came from.
I came from it too.

I loved you.
You felt like a sister.
I was your second home.

We are no longer friends
because you wanted your share of love
and you wanted mine too.

I can't stay broken;
I'm not your glue.
I can't help you
when you keep on taking.
That's not how friendship works.

When They Die Young

He chased you with a butcher knife.
He slammed you against a door of nails.
He hurt you over and over and over.
He was a villain in your story
while being a prince in mine.
I don't know how to reconcile
the things he did to you
with the love he held for me.
I love him and I still do.
I'm sorry he hurt you.

He isn't here to make amends.
I want to believe if he hadn't died at seventeen,
he would've healed.
Become the brother you deserved.

No Doormat Here

I'm not nice;
I'm kind.
One is a people pleaser;
the other stands up for herself.

Witchhood

We were all witches once.
Testing our powers,
raising our voices,
spinning our stories,
dancing in secret,
forming a sisterhood,
so that one day
we would no longer be feared
but loved as equals.

Happily

Burn bridges,
not yourself.

Father Not Like Daughter

My father once said
I'm just like him.
But all we shared was a lack of self-love.
I've shed that skin.
I might still be raw and exposed
but I'm thriving, loving myself again.

Love with No Edges

I'll never understand
not pouring into your child
like an infinity pool.

Love is an infinite resource.

Love Lesson

If I could share a love lesson,
I would tell you:

Love is beautiful, not monstrous.
The fairy tales we grew up with
failed to tell us love is not just a kiss,
a hope, a conquest.

Love is simple,
not twisted and complicated.
Show love often and mean it.
Forgetting love does more harm than good.

*Originally published in Outlying Voice anthology, Volume 7.

RENA JOY

Frog Prince, I Found Him in the Spring

I love the sound of frogs.
Their longing to be loved.
A chorus of lovers
silenced by my approach.

I've learned to be still,
lie in bed with the screen door ajar.
I stretch to hear my name.
Their springtime promise:
Kiss me; I'm your prince.

We Bought the House for Children

We bought a house for children,
but they never came
until we walked away.
Our empty tower
filled with the joy of their being.

Sweet princess kiss
pulling me from slumber.
I stumble through motherhood,
wakefulness never ending.

The Scared Cinderella

I want to write poems about love
and joy and peace.
I want to be like the other girls,
hopeful and shiny.
Dancing with their princes.

Although I'm no longer consumed
by darkness and sadness,
I'm home amongst the stars;
I'm cozy breathing in the dark.
I'm married to the one.
I'm a mother to pure joy.
I'm in harmony rocking her to sleep
and laying my head on my husband's chest.

But I'm not like the other girls.
Happily ever after isn't safe.

Unsealed

My family will never know
the healed me
because I can't talk about
the things that broke me.

In My Home We Don't Repeat Cycles

History could repeat itself
if I let it.
Silencing my daughter
with a look, a word, an action.
Passing on pain
I should've never held in the first place.
But a world with less love
doesn't sit right with me.

Safe in a Fairytale World

I'm safe here—stories unfolding
monsters
and mysteries
and mayhem.
My kind of world
where nothing is real
but what I make of it.

RENA JOY

Motherhood, My Ticket to Freedom

The last time I saw you,
my baby almost rolled off the bed
because you had your picture
and no further use for her.

The last time I heard your voice,
you asked, "have you sold your daughter yet?"
like abandonment is funny.

The last time you reached out,
you wrote,
my beautiful, talented daughter
for the world to see.
But where was the love when we were alone?

Your cruelty was our ending.
My daughter, my beginning of being free.

Is the Best Yet to Come?

I want to believe
the best is yet to come,
that there is meaning behind all this healing.
But life doesn't always have a silver lining,
so I'll take this moment to enjoy the calm,
pet my dog, snuggle my daughter,
eat a piece of cheesecake.

I'll invite my future self to dinner,
let go of what could've been.
She'll show me a changed future,
but her breath is all
the evidence I need
to start believing there is life to live
and joy to be found
after trauma.

Warrior Woman

If you are grieving your warrior woman,
I hold this space for you.
She kept you safe.
She helped you breathe
until you could survive on your own.

Maybe you feel strange
grieving a piece of you,
but change is hard and icky
and complicated.
Trust the process.
Let her rest.
Her battle cry was heard.

Sun & Moon

I'm not a coffin.
Pain will not confine me.
Secrets will not lie with me.

I'm pulling the cord,
asking to climb out.
No longer a zombie
amongst the masses.

Wash the makeup
from my face,
watch my mask slip.

No longer a phantom
singing my soul song,
whole and extraordinary.
The sun and the moon welcome me.

RENA JOY

I'm More than My Trauma But ...

Trauma isn't everything I am.
It's the helicopter parent swirling in my head.
It drops thoughts like care packages full of bombs.
It doesn't seem to matter how many times I implode,
I keep snapping the packages up.
This one has tape and glue.
I piece myself back together.
Hopefully for the last time.

Trauma isn't everything I am.
It's a roadblock I can't always clear
on my own.

The Ledge

Summer memories
of bikini tops
and shallow pools
and picnics in grass
and you beside me,
with me.

Summer memories
of skirts
and silk panties.
and beat-up trucks,
late-night drives
and windows
fresh with steam.

Summer memories
take me to the ledge.

Shooting Star

Maybe you think you're nothing.
No one would notice if you disappeared.
Maybe you've forgotten
you're a shooting star.
The world is waiting,
wishing for you
to shine once more.

-the world needs your light

Light the Way

The world needs your light.
I know this because
I've been in the dark,
treading in its depths.
If I had let it,
it would've drowned me.
I wouldn't be here writing about hope
while I snuggle my daughter to my chest.

My Anxiety Makes Me Weird

The before me
liked to pull all-nighters,
Chicken-Little-ing the world.
Every decision analyzed,
every word scrutinized,
every interaction dissected.

The now me smiles.
Sometimes winces with ghosts of past.
Most of the time, I'm happy and wholeheartedly me
with no idea of who future me will be.
That's okay.
She will live to tell the tale.

I. If Karma Could Speak

It's not fair your childhood
was spotty and scary.
It's not fair you only
had yourself.
It's not fair you didn't get the love
you deserved.
I know it's not fair.
I'm sorry.

II. If Karma Could Speak

It's not fair you've remained unseen.
It's not fair your voice was stolen.
It's not fair that far too many people witnessed
your destruction and remained unmoved.

It's not fair. It's not fair. It's not fair. It's not fair. It's not fair.
It's not fair. It's not fair. It's not fair. It's not fair. It's not fair.
It's not fair.
It's not fair.
It's not fair.

I know it's not fair.
I'm sorry.

I'll Be My Own Fate Sister

There was a time
I wished my fate string would snap,
plunging me into the after.
But now that I'm grown,
I'm my own fate sister,
cutting toxicity and
pruning back what doesn't serve me.
My fate is finally in my hands.
Never again will others determine my future.

RENA JOY

The Return of the What Ifs

What if I had been loved from the start?
What if I had known my mothers? Known myself?
What if my fathers had changed? Shown up for me?
What if I never woke up?

What if ...

My ancestors are here now holding my hand.
They whisper,
Life hasn't been fair
but what if you take another chance
and you get everything you dreamed of?

Love or Luv?

I call my husband love.
My brother-in-law grunts and curls his lip
like he just bit into an undercooked potato.
My father-in-law cracks a joke:
"Is that spelled L-O-V-E or L-U-V?"

"Whatever spelling makes you more uncomfortable,"
replies my husband.

What is it about love that makes them shift
like they have been carrying the weight of war
on their backs?

I see the way they look at their wives,
jumping up to bring them a warm cup of comfort.
I watch them play tenderly with my daughter,
getting on her level, eliciting laughs.
I know I can call them for help,
and I have more than once to jumpstart my car.

Showing love isn't the problem.
They feel it for their wives and their children
and maybe a sprinkle for me,
but that I will never be sure of
because they crack their jokes and curl their lips.

What is it about love that
they find offensive enough to call me out?
Would they rather I remain quiet
and uninvolved in a family
I want so desperately to be my home?
Would they rather I reduce him to nothingness?
Would cruelness make my love tolerable?

Don't they know if I ever stop calling him love,
then I have forgotten him?

I don't want to forget the warmth of his hand
interlaced with mine,
or the jokes zinging as we take a midnight drive.
I want to love him forever and always.
He is my L-O-V-E.

We Can Sit Together

You've witnessed my tears;
I've held you through yours.
While my load isn't for you to bear,
I will not hide my feelings from you.
Emotions are not to be feared
or dealt with alone.
I'm here for you,
showing you how to feel
in a world that has grown numb.

May I always be your safe space.

XO

Mom

Love Ever After

Promising to never hurt me isn't real
for two hearts to remain strong.
Tell me you'll never stop reaching for me,
or unlearn the sound of my heart.
Maybe then I'll start believing
we can last forever.

Inheritance

I'm at peace with who I am—
~~the hopeless girl~~,
~~the wicked girl~~,
~~the ice queen~~,
~~the damsel in distress~~,
~~the curse breaker~~.

Loving myself enough
not to stay stuck in the past,
or repeat cycles of abuse.

Moral: Sometimes tomatoes drop far from the vine.

Safety Heals Many Wounds

Once a hopeless girl,
always a hopeless girl.
(Except we both know that isn't true, right?)

Right?

Return to Sender

You met the hopeless girl (maybe you are her).
Witnessed her story unfold.
Maybe you're wondering,
will she become a hopeful girl?

The hopeless girl changed her fate.
No longer doomed to repeat her parents' past.
She is thriving in a story of her own making.
In this space, perhaps there is room now
for hope to return.

RENA JOY

FAIRY TALES FOR HOPELESS GIRLS

Thank you so much, dear readers, for joining me. I have one last poem and a story to share. November 5, 2024 my debut Almost Loved released. That evening, I took a photo outside of Chapters bookstore with a dream that I would soon have my book on their shelves. Fast forward to June 2025 (after many months of doubting myself), my dream became a reality. I wrote this poem the morning I was about to go see my debut, Almost Loved, in bookstores for the first time.

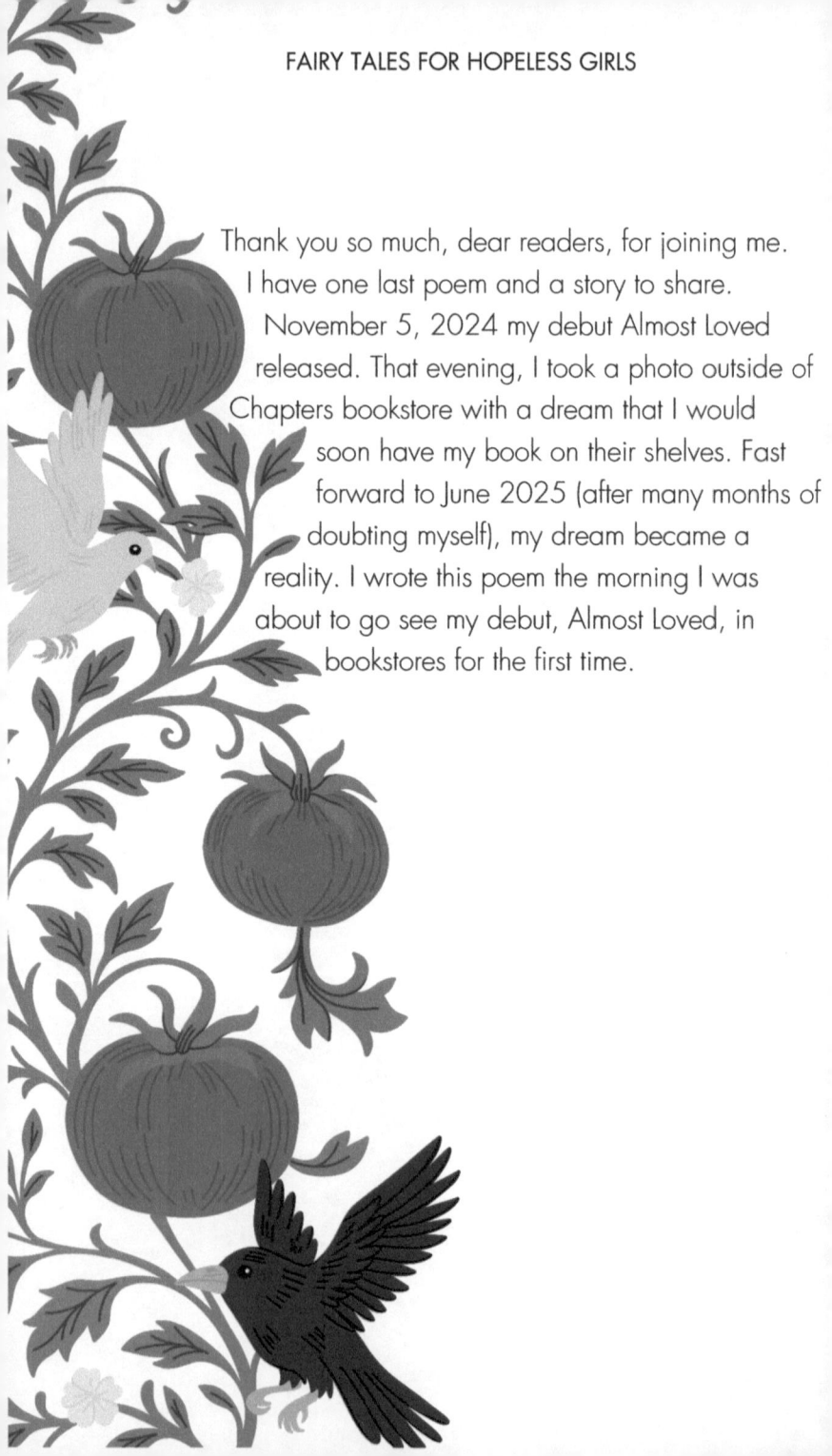

RENA JOY

Endings Are Also Beginnings

A year ago
a pair of mourning doves
nested outside my window.
For a moment, my grief lifted from my bones
and I was weightless.
I knew this sadness wouldn't last forever.

Today, I spot a crow
as I sip my morning coffee.
The fear in my chest
is as dark as his feathers
as I pick apart my new beginning.

He isn't here to tell me to be afraid.
Change is brewing.

I'm like the crow
mischievous and resourceful.
I'm like the doves
at peace and in love.

I've become a messenger
bringing hope to those who need it the most.

Acknowledgments

Thank you to my readers for making this writing journey worthwhile. I hope the poems in my book have left you feeling seen. Healing is messy and slow at times. I hope one day you'll look back and see how far you've come.

Thank you to Shelby Leigh for her editorial insight and for agreeing to work with me on another book. Thank you to my proofreader Amanda Matwie and for being a reader of my work long before we worked together.

Thank you to my illustrator Jacinta Kay. Your cover art is the chef's kiss. The frog on the spine brings me immense joy. The wolf and the girl stunning!

Thank you to the poetry community for making me believe I could, in fact, publish not one but two poetry collections. Thank you to the adoptee community for showing up for me.

Thank you to my early readers, Lily Freemark and Jonna Kihlman for their insight and encouragement. Thank you to my accountability partner Deanna Repose Oaks for the love and pep talks.

Thank you to my loves for loving me.

Thank you to me for writing this book and continuing to do the work to heal.

If you enjoyed Fairy Tales for Hopeless Girls, please consider leaving a review on Amazon, Goodreads, or Indigo. I appreciate any kind words you have to share. Thank you so much for reading.

Another great poetry book by Rena Joy

"What if you spend the rest of your life chasing love, only to find her cowering in the pit of your stomach.

When then?"

Discover Rena's debut, where she invites you to follow along with a former foster child's search for love and healing, while pushing back on the labels assigned to her at birth. Grappling with subjects of abuse, mental health, and deeply held grief, this collection aims to answer: what does it truly mean to be loved in a world where you're seen as second best? Available wherever books are sold.

Stay in touch with Rena Joy

renajoypoetry.com
TikTok @renajoypoetry
Instragram @renajoypoetry
Threads @renajoypoetry
Pinterest @renajoypoetry

Join The Joy Connection,
Rena Joy's free poetry newsletter.
Monthly letter includes behind the scenes,
bonus content and other fun stuff!

About the author

Rena Joy is from Halifax, Nova Scotia. She grew up in rural Alberta, where she now resides with her family. Poetry is her first love. She won a poetry contest in elementary and ever since has been obsessed with words. Outside of writing, Rena enjoys a quiet nerdy life surrounded by books, nature and her family.

www.renajoypoetry.com

May
you
never
remain
hopeless

www.ingramcontent.com/pod-product-compliance
Lightning Source LLC
LaVergne TN
LVHW041636060526
838200LV00040B/1596